F. W. HARVEY

F.W. HARVEY

Collected Poems 1912-1957

DOUGLAS McLEAN
THE FOREST BOOKSHOP
Coleford, Glos.

Published by Douglas McLean

at

THE FOREST BOOKSHOP

32 Market Place, Coleford, Glos. GL16 8AA

First Published
1983

ISBN 0 946252 05 X

Printed in Great Britain by
Logos Ltd.
Typesetting by 'Soluna' Typesetting Service

CONTENTS

THE POEMS

F. W. Harvey 1916

Publisher's Note

F.W. Harvey was born in 1888 and died in 1957, aged 69, at his home in Yorkley in the Forest of Dean, Gloucestershire. Although he enjoyed considerable recognition as a poet during his lifetime, popular interest in his work has faded and he has not been given the importance in our list of English poets he deserves.

He was a "War Poet", a contemporary of Siegfried Sassoon, Wilfred Owen, Ivor Gurney and Rupert Brooke. He fought in the front line trenches of Flanders and in France in the 5th Battalion of the Gloucestershire Regiment, first as a Private Soldier, then as a Commissioned Officer and he was decorated for bravery in the field. He was captured from behind their own lines by the Germans and made a prisoner of war in 1916.

His wartime poetry, much of which was written from the prison camps, was sent in regular contributions to his Battalion magazine, "The Fifth Gloucestershire Gazette", but they were not so much about death, the suffering, agony or discomfort of war, as about courage, comfort and hope. Harvey's greatness lies in his ability to seek and find beauty in a world of sadness, horror and trouble, and always to be aware of the spark of courage in himself and his fellow soldiers, kindled from thoughts of home. From a crude drawing of ducks, for example, that a fellow prisoner had painted on the prison wall, came the inspiration for his delightful and perhaps best known poem – "Ducks", which begins, "From troubles of the world I turn to ducks. . ."

He could always see beyond the trenches and the prison walls to his native Gloucestershire, of which he wrote with such beauty and delight, both during the war and in peacetime. His love for the countryside and its people, his close observation of nature and his compassion and humour gave rise to some wonderful folk poetry. His poems were soon recognised, collected and published in book form – "A Gloucestershire Lad" (1916), "Gloucestershire Friends" (1917), "Ducks and Other Verses" (1919), "Farewell" (1921), "September" (1925), etc. But since the 1950's, his works have not been reprinted, although he is often quoted in anthologies.

It is, therefore, with great pride that this publisher can now present a new collection of F.W. Harvey's work, which includes about 30 previously unpublished poems to re-introduce his important and inspiring poetry to readers of English Literature.

D.M.

FREDERICK WILLIAM HARVEY
(1888 - 1957)

Will Harvey, poet, music-lover, soldier, prisoner-of-war, sportsman, broadcaster and solicitor, was a truly remarkable son of Gloucestershire, with whom it was an honour to have walked and talked. He was one of a trio (the others being his close friends Ivor Gurney and Herbert Howells) who have done so much to enrich our lives with their music and literature.

In his vintage years, Will Harvey was a talker with a great zest for life, an original mind and an ability to set to verse so many surprising little incidents that took place around him, and often he would jot down in a note-book those that caught his eye or ear. He loved words, and even made up some, when no other one was available! But how many of us could have put into a poem such an unlikely subject as ducks (and whilst in a war-prison into the bargain)? Yet this poem of his is known throughout the world, and it was his memories of their antics on the pond in the grounds of that red brick house at Minsterworth where he spent some marvellously happy days, which prompted this little masterpiece. And what a wonderful, warm, welcoming home at Minsterworth it was! No wonder that his thoughts repeatedly turned to it when abroad in the army. There can have been few more hospitable homes in the whole of Gloucestershire than Redlands.

His love for Gloucestershire, its river, its hills and its orchards are all reflected in his writings, and after his sojourn as a prisoner-of-war in seven German camps during the 1914 - 18 war, he wrote that he had no wish ever to live away from his native county, and this wish was virtually fulfilled.

One remembers with delight the gusto with which he would sit at the piano and sing, and gleefully fit into the songs any words or ideas one could put to him whilst his playing and singing of 'Waltzing Matilda' and that sad song, 'Farewell Manchester' can never be forgotten. One remembers, too, the well-nigh violent games of table-tennis which he played with his brother, to an accompaniment of good-humoured oaths and curses.

There are memories, too, of almost his last visit to friends in Gloucester, when he sat and read to them, far into the night, some of his poems, as only he could read them. The magic of the poet Harvey was still there, and the incident brought back much earlier times when he could so easily entrance a young audience with his reading of such tales as, for instance, Brer Rabbit. He was able to extract every ounce of meaning from the words, and his own pleasure and delight were readily imparted.

Perhaps Fortune did not smile on him as amply as it should, and perhaps, too, the passing years brought some disappointments, but that strong and unique personality was with him to the end, and in so many ways he was head and shoulders above his more affluent associates.

These few thoughts are set down by one who, from the age of six, knew Will Harvey well, and who is so grateful for the friendship which existed to the end of Harvey's life. To those who knew him, it is perhaps not surprising that some of Harvey's last words, on his deathbed, were, "I have burnt myself out for the glory of Gloucestershire". How true it was! A great son of Gloucestershire, he will long be remembered. Whilst for those who do not yet know his poems, and who love this county, there are treasures awaiting them, from one who gave so much and received so little.

B.C.F.

DUCKS

To F.M., who drew them in Holzminden Prison.

I

From troubles of the world
I turn to ducks,
Beautiful comical things
Sleeping or curled
Their heads beneath white wings
By water cool,
Or finding curious things
To eat in various mucks
Beneath the pool,
Tails uppermost, or waddling
Sailor-like on the shores
Of ponds, or paddling
–Left! right!–with fanlike feet
Which are for steady oars
When they (white galleys) float
Each bird a boat
Rippling at will the sweet
Wide waterway . . .
When night is fallen *you* creep
Upstairs, but drakes and dillies
Nest with pale water-stars,
Moonbeams and shadow bars,
And water-lilies:
Fearful too much to sleep
Since they've no locks
To click against the teeth
Of weasel and fox.
And warm beneath
Are eggs of cloudy green
Whence hungry rats and lean

Would stealthily suck
New life, but for the mien,
The bold ferocious mien
Of the mother-duck.

II

Yes, ducks are valiant things
On nests of twigs and straws,
And ducks are soothy things
And lovely on the lake
When that the sunlight draws
Thereon their pictures dim
In colours cool.
And when beneath the pool
They dabble, and when they swim
And make their rippling rings,
Oh ducks are beautiful things!

But ducks are comical things:—
As comical as you.
Quack!
They waddle round, they do.
They eat all sorts of things,
And then they quack.
By barn and stable and stack
They wander at their will,
But if you go too near
They look at you through black
Small topaz-tinted eyes
And wish you ill.
Triangular and clear
They leave their curious track
In mud at the water's edge,
And there amid the sedge
And slime they gobble and peer
Saying "Quack! quack!"

III

When God had finished the stars and whirl of coloured suns
He turned His mind from big things to fashion little ones,
Beautiful tiny things (like daisies) He made, and then
He made the comical ones in case the minds of men
    Should stiffen and become
    Dull, humourless and glum:
And so forgetful of their Maker be
As to take even themselves – *quite seriously.*
Caterpillars and cats are lively and excellent puns.
All God's jokes are good – even the practical ones!
And as for the duck, I think God must have smiled a bit
Seeing those bright eyes blink on the day He fashioned it.
And He's probably laughing still
                        at the sound that came out of its bill!

THE HORSES

My father bred great horses,
    Chestnut, grey, and brown.
They grazed about the meadows,
    And trampled into town.

They left the homely meadows
    And trampled far away,
The great shining horses,
    Chestnut, and brown, and grey.

Gone are the horses
    That my father bred.
And who knows whither? . . .
    Or whether starved or fed? . . .
Gone are the horses,
    And my father's dead.

26.3.1883

March winds bugled that morn
In ear of a babe unborn:
"Up, child! March!"
Lord, I have heeded Thy horn.

F.W.H.
A Portrait

A thick-set, dark-haired, dreamy little man,
    Uncouth to see,
Revolving ever this preposterous plan –
Within a web of words spread cunningly
To tangle Life – no less,
(Could he expect success!)

Of Life, he craves not much, except to watch.
    Being forced to act,
He walks behind himself, as if to catch
The motive – an accessory to the fact,
Faintly amused, it seems,
Behind his dreams.

Yet hath he loved the vision of this world,
    And found it good:
The Faith, the fight 'neath Freedom's flag unfurled,
The friends, the fun, the army-brotherhood.
But faery-crazed or worse
He twists it all to verse!

TRIOLET

Winter has hardened all the ground,
    But flowers are on the window-pane;
No others are there to be found:—
Winter has hardened all the ground.
But here, while Earth is bare and bound,
    Bloom ghosts of those his frost has slain,
Winter has hardened all the ground,
    But flowers are on the window-pane.

SOLITARY CONFINEMENT

No mortal comes to visit me to-day,
    Only the gay and early-rising Sun
Who strolled in nonchalantly, just to say,
    "Good morrow, and despair not, foolish one!"
But like the tune which comforted King Saul
Sounds in my brain that sunny madrigal.

Anon the playful Wind arises, swells
    Into vague music, and departing, leaves
A sense of blue bare heights and tinkling bells,
    Audible silences which sound achieves
Through music, mountain streams, and hinted heather,
And drowsy flocks drifting in golden weather.

Lastly, as to my bed I turn for rest,
    Comes Lady Moon herself on silver feet
To sit with one white arm across my breast,
    Talking of elves and haunts where they do meet.
No mortal comes to see me, yet I say
"Oh, I have had fine visitors to-day!"

THE BOY WITH LITTLE BARE TOES

He ran all down the meadow, that he did,
The boy with the little bare toes,
The flowers they smelt so sweet, so sweet,
And the grass it felt so funny and wet
And the birds sang just like this – "chereep!"
And the willow-trees stood in rows.
"Ho! ho!"
Laughed the boy with the little bare toes.

Now the trees had no insides – how funny!
Laughed the boy with the little bare toes.
And he put in his hand to find some money
Or honey – yes, that would be best – oh, best!
But what do you think he found, found, found?
Why, six little eggs all round, round, round,
And a mother-bird on the nest,
Oh, yes!
The mother-bird on her nest.

He laughed "Ha! ha!" and he laughed, "He! he!"
The boy with the little bare toes.
But the little mother-bird got up from her place
And flew right into his face, ho! ho!
And pecked him on the nose, "Oh! oh!"
Yes, pecked him on the nose, "Oh! oh!"
Yes, pecked him right on the nose.
"Boo! Boo!"
Cried the boy with the little bare toes.

SONG OF MINSTERWORTH

Air: 'The Vicar of Bray'

In olden, olden centuries
    On Gloucester's holy ground, sir,
The monks did pray and chant all day,
    And grow exceeding round, sir;
And here's the reason that they throve
    To praise their pleasant fortune,
"We keep our Beasts" – thus quoth the priests,
    "In Minsterworth – that's Mortune!"[1]

So this is the chorus we will sing,
    And this is the spot we'll drink to,
While blossom blows and Severn flows,
    And Earth has mugs to clink to.

Oh! there in sleepy Summer sounds
    The drowsy drone of bees, sir,
And there in Winter paints the sun
    His patterns 'neath the trees, sir;
And there with merry song doth run
    A river full of fish, sir,
That Thursday sees upon the flood
    And Friday on the dish, sir.

So this is the chorus we will sing
    And this is the spot we'll drink to,
While blossom blows and Severn flows,
    And Earth has mugs to clink to.

The jovial priests to dust are gone,
　　We cannot hear their singing;
But still their merry chorus-song
　　From newer lips runs ringing.
And we who drink the sunny air
　　And see the blossoms drifting,
Will sit and sing the self-same thing
　　Until the roof we're lifting.

So this is the chorus we will sing,
*　　And this is the spot we'll drink to,*
While blossom blows and Severn flows,
*　　And Earth has mugs to clink to.*

1. The ancient name of the parish was Mortune – that is the village in the mere; and the name was changed to Minsterworth early in the fourteenth century, because it belonged to the Minster or Abbey of Gloucester, and was the Minster's 'Worth' or farm where the cattle were kept. *F.W.H.*

THE WEAVER

Apprenticed was I
　　In days of old
To dreams held preciously
　　As bright gold.

And though none give me
　　To-day a crust,
Dreams I will weave me
　　Till I am dust.

LINCOLN'S INN FIELDS

In Lincoln's Inn Fields where you chiefly find
Law students, tramps, and babies, comes the wind
Out of the west: and straight way brings to me
Large visions of my dear, my own country.

Dear city of mine I see you like a dream
Below blue hills which shadow you and seem
Sentinels of the peace which comes to me
When I am in my dear, my own country.

High Lassington I see your woods again
Blown all about and wet with falling rain,
What Druid spell have you cast over me
Sweet woodlands of my dear, my own country.

And you dear home of mine that in my dreams
I visit. And all you my pretty streams
That dream and shine by many a shivering tree
In the dim meadows of my dear, my own country.

The great farm horses splashing in the pool
Shrill with delight of birds, the coppice cool;
These things the friendly wind brings here to me
For tokens of my dear, my own country . . .

IN FLANDERS

I'm homesick for my hills again –
My hills again!
To see above the Severn plain
Unscabbarded against the sky
The blue high blade of Cotswold lie;
The giant clouds go royally
By jagged Malvern with a train
Of shadows. Where the land is low
Like a huge imprisoning O
I hear a heart that's sound and high,
I hear the heart within me cry:
"I'm homesick for my hills again –
    My hills again!
Cotswold or Malvern, sun or rain!
    My hills again!"

SONG OF HEALTH

For friends to stand beside, for foes to fight,
For devil's work to break, for Wrong and Right,
And will (however hard) to choose between them:
For merry tales, no matter where you glean them:
Songs, stars, delight of birds, and summer roses,
Sunshine, wherein my friend the dog now dozes:
Danger – the zest of life, and Love, the lord
Of Life and Death: for every open word
Spoken in blame or praise by friend o' mine
To spur me on: for old, good memories,

Keeping in my soul's cellar like good wine:
For Truth that's strong, and Beauty so divine:
For animals, and children, and for trees,
Both wintry-black and blossoming in white:
For homely gardens and for humming bees:
For drink, and dreams, and daisies on the sod,
Plain food, and fire (when it will light) –
Thank God!

GLOUCESTERSHIRE FROM ABROAD

On Dinny Hill the daffodil
Has crowned the years returning.
The water cool in Placket Pool
Is ruffled up and burning
In little wings of fluttering fire.
And all the heart of my desire
Is now to be in Gloucestershire.

The river flows, the blossom blows
In orchards by the river.
O now to stand in that, my land,
And watch the withies shiver!
The yearning eyes of my desire
Are blinded by a twinkling fire
Of turning leaves in Gloucestershire.

The shadows fleet o'er springing wheat.
Which like green water washes
The red old earth of Minsterworth
And ripples in such flashes
As by their little harmless fire
Light the great stack of my desire
This day to be in Gloucestershire.

CRICKET: THE CATCH

Whizzing, fierce, it came
    Down the summer air,
Burning like a flame
    On my fingers bare,
And it brought to me
As swift – a memory.

Happy days long dead
    Clear I saw once more.
Childhood that is fled:
    Rossall on the shore
Where the sea sobs wild
Like a homesick child.

Oh, the blue bird's fled!
    Never man can follow.
Yet at times instead
    Comes this scarlet swallow,
Bearing on its wings
    (Where it skims and dips,
    Gleaming through the slips)
Sweet Time-strangled things.

AT AFTERNOON TEA
(Triolet)

We have taken a trench
    Near Combles, I see,
Along with the French.
We have taken a trench.
(Oh, the bodies, the stench!)
Won't you have some more tea?
    We have taken a trench
Near Combles, I see.

A POET'S INSTRUCTIONS

Dedicated to the Memory of Four London Navvies

(Tom's verse)

Before electric drills
Brought life (and modern art) its silly, hectic thrills,
I watched a lovely petal
Of men and metal
Bloom (like a daisy-flower) in Piccadilly,
And learned my poetry from it willy-nilly.

(Dick's verse)

Breathless I watched
Tom, Dick, Bill, Harry, and "another" matched
To – for one mad hour
The florets of a flower
Whose rise was that "another" with a drill
Turning and squatting – him they seemed to kill.

(Bill's verse)

I heard (aghast) the chime
Of Tom, Dick, Bill, and Harry beating time
No jerk, no hustle,
A ripple of moving muscle
Missing the little man whose moving wrist
Gave to his drill that fraction of a twist.

(Harry's verse and mine)

Disciplined loveliness
Fronted wherewith a poet need confess
Humility: an art achieved with pain
Which shows no strain –
(And folk who see the rhythmic, swinging fools,
Murmur "a happy accident!" – the fools!)

IF WE RETURN (Rondeau)

If we return, will England be
Just England still to you and me?
The place where we must earn our bread?
We, who have walked among the dead.
And watched the smile of agony,

And seen the price of Liberty,
Which we have taken carelessly
From other hands. Nay, we shall dread,
If we return,

Dread lest we hold blood-guiltily
The things that men have died to free.
Oh, English fields shall blossom red
For all the blood that has been shed
By men whose guardians are we,
If we return.

HARVEST HOME

My heart is filled with you
As a field tilled which grew
But couch and weed;
You are my cornfield spread,
Ripe to be harvested
For bitter need.

You have built barns in my heart.
You have become a part
Of all I knew:
Wherefore I dance and sing
And fear not anything
Sharp scythes may do.

THAT I MAY BE TAUGHT THE GESTURE OF HEAVEN

God of the steadfast line,
Who laid the curving Cotswolds on the sky;
God of the hills,
And of the lonely hollows in the hills,
And of the cloudy nipples of the mountains:
Teach me thy passionate austerity!
God of elm twigs
And of all winter trees
Etched ebony on sunset, or bright silver
Upon hard morning heavens;
Cunning shaper of ferns,
And ferns which whitely gleam on frosty windows
And snow-flakes:
God of the naked body beautifully snatched
To some swift-gestured loveliness of Heaven:
Master
Of stars,
And all beneath most passionately curbed
In Form: catch up my sprawling soul and fix it
In gesture of its lost divinity!

THE TREASURY

I have such joy in my heart's coffer,
Little I care what life may offer.

Little it matters if I lie
In dungeons, who possess the sky.

The sparkling morn, the starry night,
Are locked away for my delight;

And in my heart there hangs a key
To open them, called Memory.

How should I ever lack a friend
Who so have lovers without end?

How can I ever lose my home
Who bear it with me where I come?

My home is in my heart, and there
These dreadful days I do repair;

And I have broken off the seal
Of that Dream-box whose dreams are real;

So rich am I, I do possess
Their overpowering loveliness;

And have such joy in my heart's coffer,
Little I care what Life may offer.

ART AND LIFE
(A Reflection)

Design needs background – as those
    Stark trees their sky:
Or the mist that froze
    To fern upon my window delighting the eye.
Life needs Death: Earth, Heaven for circumference:
    And lacking, are jumbled jigsaws,
Sans soul, sans sense.

VIMPANY'S ROSES – A MEMORY

Not "pretty", but wildly beautiful are the red roses
Rambling over the roof of that good man's home.
Good man, I say,
So to let roses have their lovely way.
Give freely to all their hearty, heavenly welcome;
A proof that beauty was in his soul: no dread
That the clamberers might spoil that roof of his stone homestead.
(The devil take such cowardly selfishness!)
Benefactor he, to poets, and all with eyes in their head!

THE HEART'S HARVEST

So peacefully thrilling Heart's September is,
    So quiet her deep thought:
As the gleam of a dream that Life's last ember is
    To brighten a house Youth bought.

T'was Youth's tempestuous hand that scattered the seeds,
    Fruitage fulfilled the daring,
Let me now call to mind brave spring-time deeds
    And generous sharing.

Taste, test and store against the winter cold
    My apples of memory;
Sample dream-cider: better growing old
    Stranger to strengthen me!

EPITAPH

This little girl
In brown earth lies,
She shall sweeten the sweet air
Of Paradise
With her slow lovely speech
And wondering eyes.

ADOLESCENCE

This tender scorn, this majesty of weather
    Mocks all we dream or do.
Its silent message like an eagle's feather
    Flutters from out the blue
        Shaming all high endeavour,
        Making our labour vain for ever and ever.

Oh, that a quest noble enough could be found
    To match such scornful beauty!
Oh, that, with feet set firm on common ground,
    Man might attain the height of heavenly duty:
        That the green hedge into green fire
        Would flame and burn our world to Heaven's desire!

COUNTRYMAN

A boy looked over Windy Ridge,
    (Say, could that boy be I?)
He was afar the sprinkled lights
Of a city that seemed on frosty nights
A city of stars: and the forest heights
Gloomed dreary, and Windy Ridge
    Dreariest under the sky.

A man gazed back on Windy Ridge.
    "Noble and calm its line,
Star-crowned! But grooved with silly care
The faces in this tawdry flare
Of lamps. Would God I breathed sweet air
Again" (he cried) "on Windy Ridge!"
    (Say, can the voice be mine?)

THE IMPRISONED CHILD

Where's that child – ah, where –
    The child I buried *alive*
        Within me?

So long ago it was, yet there
    Trying in vain to win me
        He is crying.
    And I too cry and strive,
        Child, to win you.

O hark, hark thro' the dark
    Piteous comes his weak thin cry,
        Tiny trumpet of doom –
        "Excĕpt you become. . ."!

    O Father on high,
    Suffer *my*. . .
    Suffer *Thy* child,
    Suffer to come unto Thee
    My little child, and let him never die,
    So shall not I.

A SONG

This harp I found
        Hung on the tree of Despair;
There blossomed a lovely rose
        In the garden of care.

Under black skies
        Flitted the golden bee
Of Song: and hives of Pain
        Brim with wild honey.

THE SNOW-MAN SPEAKS

Clap hands: dance in a ring!
'Tis I will be your clown.
Take me, and make me happy as never before:
For tired I am of slow stars circling,
    And the silver crown
That sparkles upon the brows of mountains hoar.

Clap hands and dance! Maybe
    Not for a thousand years,
Children, shall I be again a foolish snow-man.
My flesh is of the clouds, and carelessly
    They scatter it down – litter for polar bears:
Cold crowns on heights unclimbed by child or man or woman.

Was it a thousand years ago – that day,
    When (dimly I remember!)
I was a snow-man before . . . such laughter rang:
Such tiny fingers patted me in play?
    Till Sun's red ember
Flamed up, and on to Everest I sprang.

Push in your bits of coal to be my eyes;
    And a red flannel rag
To flap from my white face like a scarlet tongue.
Give me an old umbrella of monstrous size.
    Is that a sugar-bag?
Then crown me! Let the festive hymn be sung!

CHRIST AND THE FAIRIES

For mortal man was Jesus born
    On Christmas Day in the morning.
For mortals was our Saviour born
    Long, long ago.

The beasts were at His bearing:
    On them He put no scorning.
Cattle lay in the stable.
    Long, long ago.

So never doubt that fairies
    On Christmas Day in the morning;
Gnomes, lepricauns, and fairies
    Long, long ago,

With kings, and those dumb oxen
    On whom He put no scorning,
Came flocking on His birthday,
    Long, long ago;

Singing fairy tunes
    On Christmas Day in the morning;
Smoothing out the straw,
    Long, long ago.

EASTER DAY
NAUGHTS AND CROSSES

"I wish those bloody men had not crucified God."
It was a bad example, and has become a bad habit.
And now we are all left bloody and horrible;
    Every one of us.

    Finding new ways of doing it
        Sleeping and waking:
    Unable to think of anything else
        In a living nightmare.

Shall we not wake from it: break from it?
Shall not the crooked cross to crown a God discrowned
Be twisted round
Some Easter – now?

Or . . .
Must it go on –
This cruel, stupid game of
            Naughts and Crosses?

JOY WITHOUT CAUSE

What lovely piping charms my thought?
    To what enticing stream
Wanders a young uncaught
    And light-foot dream?

Oh joy without a cause
    Visiting men betimes
In scorn of reason's heavy laws
    Ringing mad chimes!

Tomorrow I shall be agen
Behind the prison bars
A man of clay with other men
Peering up at stars.

Let me not quite forget
Though I must forget almost
How my feet in the Milky Way were wet
When I danced with the starry host!

HIS OWN DEAR LAND (A Song)

Cotswold curving: jagged Malvern
Drawn to God's great plan.
Shadowy Forest: shining flood-shore:
Where's best home for a man?

Where's best home? The plums glow golden
And red in Evesham's vale
In Minsterworth neither silvery fish
Nor fruit shall ever fail.

Hereford hops twine gracefully
Their tendrils. A poet fills
Long rythms of red ploughland.
Wye's wandering silver spills.

Blue hill, brown vale, green forest,
Red earth, or golden sand,
Choose! But be sure a man's best home
Lies in his own dear land.

Wander the wide world over
    (For Youth's the time to roam),
Come back a truer lover
    To – wherever was your home.

And if the dream you're seeking
    Shines in this Western sod,
Kneel down upon it, and with no speaking
    Thank your God!

CLOUDS

This Sunday morning
    I will not go to Mass.
I will not do anything
    But lie in the grass.
And watch the great clouds pass
    Moving with a slow majesty
And peace unknown, high, high,
    Above the world of men and church bells calling
    On fields of the infinite blue . . .
Where is God sending them? and to
    Do what? (I wonder)
    Rain, hail, snow, thunder?
        Or can it be
        That He
Thought on such men as lie
    Like me this sunny morning
In grass watching the sky,
    And blew them humorously
    Like bubbles out
To please such little children and truants from school
        And make them shout:
"O God! how wonderful! how wonderful!"

EASTER

Come, Angels, sing! Let music wake
And break upon the shores of Time.
For joy of the world's new-risen King!
Out of the darkness of death He brake
As at the trumpet of the spring
Violets waken and primroses pale
And all sweet flowers that fill the vale.
Those flowers sweet will die, but He
Shall blossom through eternity.

AFTER LONG WANDERING

I will go back to Gloucestershire,
To the spot where I was born,
To the talk at eve with men and women
And song on the roads at morn.
And I'll sing as I tramp by dusty hedges
Or drink my ale in the shade
How Gloucestershire is the finest home
That the Lord God ever made.

First I will go to the ancient house
Where Doomsday book was planned,
And cool my body and soul in shade
Of pillars huge which stand
Where the organ echoes thunder-like
Its paean of triumph and praise
In a temple lovely as ever the love
Of Beauty's God did raise.

Gargoyles will thrust out heads to hearken,
    A frozen forest of stone
Echo behind me as I pass
    Out of the shadow alone
To buzz and bustle of Barton Fair
    And its drifting droves of sheep,
To find three miles away the village
    Where I will sleep.

Minsterworth, queen of riverside places
    (Save Framilode, who can vie?),
To her I'll go when day has dwindled
    And the light low in the sky;
And my troubles shall fall from me, a bundle,
    And youth come back again,
Seeing the smoke of her houses and hearing
    The talk of Minsterworth men.

I'll drink my perry and sing my song
    Of home and home again,
Pierced with the old miraculous pleasure
    Keen as sharpest pain;
And if I rise to sing on the morrow
    Or if I die in my bed,
'Tis all the same: I'll be home again,
    And happy alive or dead.

SONG OF MALVERN

Some men go to Malvern
To climb the jagged rocks
That stand so high against the sky
The clouds seem wandering flocks:
Drifting flocks whose fleece
Gleams over heaven and hill,
A vision of silver peace
When the birds of the world are still.

I found peace at Malvern
And it wasn't in a rock;
It wasn't in any silver fleece
Of the wind's wandering flock;
It wasn't in the earth below
Nor in the heavens above,
Only on Malvern, years ago,
I met my love.

THE BOND

Once, I remember, when we were at home
I had come into church, and waited late,
Ere lastly kneeling to communicate
Alone: and thinking that you would not come.

Then, with closed eyes (having received the Host)
I prayed for your dear self, and turned to rise;
When lo! beside me like a blessed ghost –
Nay, a grave sunbeam – you! Scarcely my eyes
Could credit it, so softly had you come
Beside me as I thought I walked alone.

Thus long ago; but now, when fate bereaves
Life of old joys, how often as I'm kneeling
To take the Blessed Sacrifice that weaves
Life's tangled threads, so broken to man's seeing,
Into one whole; I have the sudden feeling
That you are by, and look to see a face
Made in fair flesh beside me, and all my being
Thrills with the old sweet wonder and faint fear
As in that sabbath hour – how long ago! –
When you had crept so lightly to your place.
Then, then, *I know*
(My heart can always tell) that you are near.

DRESS

That dress is fine, which doth betray
    The beauty it would hide away.
What sense is fired with fine array?

White breasts, eyes changing as the sea,
    And lovely limbs – these too may be
Clothes that but hide what's best to see:–

– A dress worn but to hide away
    The beauty which it should betray;
The form beneath the fine array.

Fine clothes are less than bodies; so
    Bodies than that we strive to know;
Which hides beneath those breasts of snow.

And so that beauty's best, I say,
    Which ever planneth to betray
The loveliness it hides away.

LUCKY

Lucky to live
    Lucky again
To have met and marched
    With the finest men
(So I believe)
    Earth ever bred
Since heaven was arched...
    But they are dead.

Lucky to love,
    Most lucky to
Have loved, of all
    I might have, you
Whom Time doth prove
    Most tender-hearted
And beautiful...
    But we are parted.

BEAUTY

Does beauty come to you
    Out of brave things?
Does beauty come to you
    From a thrush that sings?

Does beauty come to you
    Out of hammers clanging?
Does beauty come to you
    From a God hanging?

Rhythm of hammers clanging
Utter quietness of God hanging
Trilling of thrush
Dawn blush?

Does beauty come to you
Out of the air:
Everywhere?
Does it? For it is there.

I LOVE THESE THINGS

All things which bend but do not break
Before the storm; increasing
Their loveliness: the willow tree
Beautifully bending and swaying to rain
And wind unceasing.

Lilac with heart-shaped leaves – (To me
Symbol of human hearts so weak
Yet bearing tenderly the storm of Time
Préserving, still grace, and beauty of courage,
Ánd tranquillity that lit young Life's sweet face).
All things which gracefully bend but do not break
I love.

And I would bend not break:
Learn lilac-lore, and as a willow rod
Be beautiful though weak –
Obedient to the winds of the will of God.

A POET'S LOVE-SONG

(For music and to my wife, 15.8.56)

Breathe o'er my verse, dear:
    Bid the cold words glow!
    Know them as ember, dear,
    Which kindles as you blow
    To vision. Live again, dear,
    Our love of long ago!
Breathe over our dreams, dear.

TRIOLET

If Beauty were a mortal thing
    That died like laughter, grief, and lust,
The poet would not need to sing.
If Beauty were a mortal thing
It would not wound us with its sting.
    We should lie happy in the dust
If Beauty were a mortal thing
    That died like laughter, grief, and lust.

A SONG

Oh, Cranham ways are steep and green
    And Cranham woods are high,
And if I was that black rook,
    It's there that I would fly.

But since I'm here in London town,
    A silly walking man;
I'll make this song and caw it
    As loudly as I can.

PONDERING HER LOVELINESS

Pondering her loveliness
    I saw the world of sense dissolve, to take
Swift beauty in a cup
    Brimming with dreams.

Lo, as earth faded,
Line into line wondrously marrying,
Crept forth her loveliness.
    And else was nothing.

. . . . .

How frail are dreams!
The crackle of a stick beneath the heel:
The trilling of a bird,
    Shatter them, scatter them!

TO HIS MAID

Since above Time, upon Eternity
    The lovely essence of true loving's set,
Time shall not triumph over you and me,
    Nor – though we pay his debt –
Shall Death hold mastery.

Your eyes are bright for ever. Your dark hair
    Holds an eternal shade. Like a bright sword
Shall flame the vision of your strange sweet ways,
    Cleaving the years: and even your smallest word,
Lying forgotten with the things that were,
Shall glow and kindle, burning up the days.

"LOCAL FATALITIES ARE REPORTED"

Dangerously sheltered they,
The lovers lay
Upon the great dead hill,
Frail flesh and blood:
Beneath a twisted thorn,
Which to the heaven's mood
Died and was born
Again, as lightning fell.

Two mites of trembling clay –
    Ah, what cared they!
    The lightning flashed:
        They laughed.
    The thunder crashed:
        They kissed.
    The grey rain lashed
The hill: and hid them in mist.

Did they return again
To the sunny plain,
To spite and scorn,
The plane of mortal care?
Nay, with passions of skies
They mingled were . . .
They were made wise
Beneath the twisted thorn.

THE BUGLER

God dreamed a man;
Then, having firmly shut
Life like a precious metal in his fist,
Withdrew, His labour done. Thus did begin
Our various divinity and sin.
For some to ploughshares did the metal twist,
And others – dreaming empires – straightway cut
Crowns for their aching foreheads. Others beat
Long nails and heavy hammers for the feet
Of their forgotten Lord. (Who dare to boast
That he is guiltless?) Others coined it: most
Did with it – simply nothing. (Here, again,
Who cries his innocence?) Yet doth remain
Metal unmarred, to each man more or less,
Whereof to fasion perfect loveliness.

For me, I do but bear within my hand
(For sake of Him our Lord, now long forsaken)
A simple bugle such as may awaken
With one high morning note a drowsing man:
That wheresoe'er within my motherland
The sound may come, 'twill echo far and wide
Like pipes of battle calling up a clan,
Trumpeting men through beauty to God's side.

SEPTEMBER

She walketh like a ghost,
      Lovely and gray
And Faint, faint, faint . . .
      Ere Autumn's host
Of colours gay
      Breaks on the year, September
Comes sighing her soft plaint,
      "Remember!"

Remember what? All fair
      Warm loves now wan:
All fleet, fleet, fleet
      Flowers in the hair
Of Summers gone!
      Though fruit break rosy, of these
Are her most sweet
      Sad memories.

Most faint and tender
      Music awaketh,
Sighing, sighing, sighing,
      A voice to lend her.
Surely it breaketh
      Even Death's heart, as he goes
To gather in Summer's long-dying
      Last rose.

So drifting like a ghost,
      Lovely with dream
And faint, faint, faint,
      Sighing "remember," almost
September did seem
      My gray soul's image, as she
Whispered over that plaint
      So musically!

NOVEMBER

He has hanged himself – the Sun.
He dangles
A scarecrow in thin air.
He is dead for love – the Sun;
He who in forest tangles
Wooed all things fair

That great lover – the Sun,
Now spangles
The wood with blood-stains.

He has hanged himself – the Sun.
How thin he dangles
In these gray rains!

SUNSET

Night shuts from eye of man
Familiar hills and meadows
Less magically than
These strange sunset-shadows.

When up that hill I came
It was not gold, I swear:
And the off horse was lame
In the team ploughing there.

But now doth the rough world don
A robe of splendid lies:
Or painfully have I gone,
And blind, through paradise?

For there, a golden shadow,
Lieth the little hill
A smooth purple meadow
Two golden horses till.

BIRD-SONG

What know these forest birds of ours
Better than all men know?
Is life a thing of sun and flowers?
A careless, easy song? Ah, no!
Birds have their cares be sure; must win
With toil their crumbs, or shrink to skin
And bone. This Autumn air is chill
And winter comes relentlessly
With blade of ice ground keen to kill.
Hunger and death he knows, yet he –
The black-bird there, flutes still
Upon his holly tree . . .
Pours still his liquid lovely phrases:
His confident, courageous phrases,
As if 'twere buttercups and daisies
Beneath him grew.
They are all dead. Beneath my feet
The frosty grass is stiff and white:–
Even as old age. But if I knew
The secret of that song's delight,
Old age and death might both seem sweet.

PLUMP PEARS (Triolet)

Plump pears are plumping on the ground.
(And Father said we must not pick them.)
We didn't. Rough-boy-Wind rushed round
And plumped those pears upon the ground.
Hark to him – what a lovely sound!
He cannot eat, nor even lick them.
We can, since they are on the ground,
Though Father said we weren't to *pick* them.

RICH SNAIL!

Rich snail to carry on your back
    So beautiful an house!
You leave behind a shining track
    For path you need not use.

Slowly you creep your life away
    Having small need to travel
(And nothing in rent nor rate to pay
Nor "Planner" to tell you "yea" or "nay")
    Gliding on garden gravel.

You're welcome to crawl here at will
    No poet here illtreats you. . .
But thresh-flail-thrush with cruel bill
    Bashes your home – and EATS YOU!

And did a bomb descend here now,

I'd fare no better (snail) than thou,
    Poor snail.
    Poor *male*!

ELVERS

Up the Severn River from Lent to Eastertide
Millions and millions of slithy elvers glide,
Millions, billions of glassy bright
      Little wormy fish,
            Chewed-string fish,
                  Slithery dithery fish,
In the dead of night.

Up the gleaming river miles and miles along
Lanterns burn yellow: old joke and song
Echo as fishermen dip down a slight
      Wide frail net,
            Gauzy white net,
                  Strong long net
In the water bright.

From the Severn river at daybreak come
Hundreds of happy fishermen home
With bags full of elvers: perhaps that's why
      We all love Lent
            Lean mean Lent,
                  Fishy old Lent,
When the elvers fry.

When elvers fry for breakfast with egg chopped small
And bacon from the side that's hung upon the wall.
When the dish is on the table how the children shout
      "Oh, what funny fish,
            Wormy squirmy fish,
                  Weeny white fish,
Our mother's dishing out!"

Eels have a flavour (and a baddish one) of oil.
"When we have shuffled *down* their mortal coil,
What dreams may come!" what horrid nightmares neigh,
Gallop or squat,
Trample or trot,
Vanishing not
Till break of day!

"Never start nothing," says the motto in our pub:
"It might lead to summat": that's (as Shakespeare said) the rub!
So I'm not going to tell you, anyway not yet,
If the elvers are eels,
White baby eels,
Tiny shiny eels,
Caught with a net –

Or another quite separate wriggly kind of grub,
For I've seen more fights over that outside a pub
Than ever *you* saw at Barton Fair when Joe
The brown gipsy man,
The tawny gipsy man,
The tipsy gipsy man,
Tried to smart up the show.

But anyway, good people, you may search the river over
Before a breakfast tastier or cheaper you discover
Than elvers, and if all the year the elver season lasted
I wouldn't mind a bit,
I wouldn't care a bit,
Not a little tiny bit,
How long I fasted!

THE LANTERN OF THE HILL

Sailors and soldiers weary
Of wandering afar
Where shines the light to steer ye
Homeward like the Star?

Where shines it? Surely on Viney,
Beaconing, beckoning home;
Do not old memories twine ye
Like tendrils of vine as ye come?

To the Faith and the Forest that bred ye –
Men no more to roam
Hath not this lantern led ye?
Home?

The church, lantern-like "glowing";
A flag of faith unfurled,
Stands it not still there showing
"The Light of the World"!

SONG

Some meet love in a cinema
And some at a chapel door,
And some just meet in the jostling street
And some on a gay dance-floor.

But I met my queen in the Forest of Dean
Where no street lamps are lighted
And both quite lost mid gloomy green
We roamed – two babes benighted –

’Till her home was reached in a deep-sunk glade,
    And just for doing my duty
Her parents a hero out of me made
    And (Thanks to a forest of beauty)
Yes, thanks to the dark old Forest of Dean
We are wedded, and happy as king or queen!

AFTERTHOUGHT

The comical beauty of ducks:
The snowy glory of swans:
Wrens’ twitter and thrushes’ trill:
    Escapism! – so, you sneer.
What do *you* escape *from* or *to*?
What, and how do you do?
    Realities! And so what?
Molecules to you.
Realities:– The city man’s watch and seal!
But for me the seal of the ocean.
Snail-trail-opalescent-house-moving.
Pulling horses: and ploughland in long lines of verse behind them,
Whence loveliness of windy wheat in the fall.
    – To you all molecules.
Notwithstanding (molecules to you) I will praise beauty and wonder
Of common things and loveliness that rejoices ever
My heart:– *not yours*?
    Molecules to you!

MY VILLAGE

I love old Minsterworth. I love the trees:
And when I shut my eyes they are most clear,
Those leafy homes of wren and red-breast dear,
Those winter traceries so black and light.
I love the tangled orchards blowing bright
With clouds of apple blossom, and the red
Ripe fruit that hangs a-shining in blue air
Like rubies hanging in the orchard's hair.

I love old Minsterworth. I love the river
Where elver fishers bend with twinkling lights
And salmon catchers spend their fruitful nights.
I love the sleek brown skin, the mighty rush,
The angry head upreared, the splendid hush
When the Great Bore (grown breathless) 'ere he turns
Catches his wind; and nothing on the thick
Tide moves; and you can hear your watch's tick.

I love old Minsterworth. I love the men:
The fishers and the cider-makers and
All who laugh and labour on that land
With humour and long patience loved of God.
I love the harmless gossips all a-nod,
The children bird-like, and the women old
Like wrinkled crab-apples: and I will pray –
God save old Minsterworth, and such, for aye.

A WALKER'S REFLECTION

(Written on Primrose Hill, May 7, 1949)

That fern – that force,
Pushing its baby crozier-frond thro' concrete!
Yet no more (seen to be believed) marvellous
Than spread of widening Severn,
Speeding to Avonmouth below these hills,
Palette of mingled hues in misty morn:
Or jargon of jubilant bird song
Colour and song and shine.
How to describe? – A peacock's tail-feather as glimpsed thro' smoke?
But 'tis impossible. May God bless the words
I write, resting awhile in quiet of a little church, transmute and glorify!
Making them a worthy mantle for May,
The month of Mary.

THE PATH OF THE STORM

Half of our trees were white;
    That was on the windward side,
Where the blast blew fast for a day and a night
    Leaving dark or snowy bark for guide
To the points of the compass.
Dark was the bark on the east,
Dark as a pansy petal
    But westward whence the storm did race
The bark was shining metal.
    One side of each tree was bright
The other dark as night.
    Westward, was shining metal
Eastward, a pansy petal.

POEMS FOR THREE SISTERS

For Anne

IN WAR TIME

The bluebells chime in Pillowell
    For lovers to be wed.
They chime unheard save of the bird
    That carols overhead.

White May-bloom falls in Pillowell
    As showering on a bride,
    But in the trees there sighs a breeze
    For the seas that are so wide.

Oh, when agen in Pillowell
    Shall greet the lovers?
That not breeze nor bell nor trees
    Nor bird discovers.

For Rosemary

ASK LIFE

Ask not the clock
What is the meaning
Of its "tick tock".
Content be you, as I, to mark the sliding
Of Time. No chime
Breaks Life, now gliding
Quietly through our dream "forget-me-nots."
Ask meaning
Only of Life, the river which flows forever,
Bearing away into Eternity
Soul-Boats!

For June

SONNET (UPON AN APPLE TREE IN WINTER)

Our apple tree now flaunts its plumes of snow
Pround of its frozen beauty: proud to be bare;
Barren of fruit and leafage: yet as fair
In winter as in spring and autumn. Lo,
Frozen in loveliness she standeth now
Forgetting how bright blossoms crowned her head,
Only the robin minds her of the red
And luscious fruit that hung upon her bough.
Oh wise and happy tree that doth not grieve
For what is over, and with gratitude
Takes present life though frozen life it be;
Knowing all seasons breathe beatitude:
Forseeing future spring and autumn glee:–
Would man might so *Accept; Endure; Believe.*

CHARLIE "THE BLACK"

A Tribute

Charlie, "the black," and Christ, Our Lord,
Lived lives that ran in strange accord:
And spent them mostly on the road.

Christ would not think it blasphemy
To point this similarity,
For spake He not: "Come, follow Me"?

Homeless were both, as we do know.
Harmless were both, as time did show.
No hoarded gold had they, I trow!

Both country-lovers; both keen-eyed;
Pondering oft through countryside
How lambs and lilies lived and died.

Christ washed the feet of disciples twelve,
Charlie cleaned boots and shoes for pelf
Enough (sometimes) to feed himself.

Christ the King at Christmastide
Was born in a stable with no pride.
'Twas in a stable Charlie died.

So sang he his *"Nunc Dimittis"*
And entered into palaces
Reserved for spirits such as his.

And we may glory as we scan
A likeness of our Lord in man,
And strive to copy as we can:

And hear again, with no dismay,
The trumpeting of an ancient lay:
"He hath exalted the humble and meek,
And the rich He hath sent empty away."

All Hallows Eve.

HYMN FOR ARMISTICE DAY

Of yellow poplars flickering like tall
Candles before a shrine; of leaves that fall
Like blood; and of old English oaks that stand
Black against sunset down and up the land,
Think thou to-day.

Of men gone singing down to death, for whom
This English pageant pleads till day of doom:
Gay hearts of England, than old oak more strong,
Who died for a dream of England, righting wrong:
Think thou to-day.

Of sighing willows bending to a pool
Which golden light makes calm and beautiful
As Death: of streams which run so joyously
Down to the one, to the eternal sea:
Dream thou to-day.

* * *

For our rich-memoried England, and for them
Who crowned her with their lives' bright diadem:
For lover's eyes washed clear by grief and pride:
With humble heart unto the Crucified
Pray thou to-day.

LYDNEY TO COLEFORD (By Rail)

All creeping things the Lord God made.
    And thus 'tis demonstrated
A railway-line may be divine;
    This engine God-created:–
This thing which wakes and sleeps again,
Which crawls and stops and creeps again,
Up slopes and into deeps again,
    Through forest shine and shade.

Is yon the driver? *Driver!* Nay!
    'Tis one who leads, I wist,
Upon his crazy way and mazy
    Some dark Somnambulist,
Within whose dim and sleep drugged brain
Thoughts move. *Call not this dream a train!*
This sleeping-beauty, sweetly fain
    To loiter through a day.

Who would *not* loiter? Here the bracken
    Gleams green and densely spread,
Here call the birds their pretty words
    In leafage overhead.
A butterfly has kept with me
His innocent wavering company
For miles: at moments *slept with me*
    Whenas our pace did slacken.

Abandon hope all ye who here
    Enter to keep appointment!
A gift more fair, a gift more rare,
    A kind and healing ointment,
This train provides. Then cast away
Dull care, and for a Summer's day
Ignore as dross Time's "Yea" and "Nay",
    Discard Life's fret and fear.

Too oft doth hurry rule us. Let
    For once the tumult fade:
Fade into humming of bees coming
    Sweet-laden down a glade:
Fade into glint of fern and flower,
Where quarries gleam and foxgloves tower,
And for one lovely lazy hour
    Forget – forget – forget.

You *will* arrive – impatient ass –
    Too soon! and then alighting
Meet kith and kin and wag a chin
    O'er wrongs past human righting.
Discuss old strife; new scandal: – such
Soft social soot as serves to smutch
A life once tuned to Nature touch
    Now seldom felt – alas!

TO OLD COMRADES, A FOREST OFFERING

Knowing that war was foul, yet all a-hunger
For that most dear companionship it gave,
I wished myself once more on lousy straw;
And in a trice was there, and ten years younger,
With singing soldiers scornful of the grave:
The tough mates, the rough mates that lay on lousy straw,
And since have laid them down in earth . . .
            I saw
Again their faces flicker in the light
Of candles fixed most dangerously in rings
Of bayonets stabbed in wooden beams, or stuck
Down into the floor's muck . . .

            The woods are bright
With smouldering beech. Only a robin sings.
Alone to-day amid the misty woods,
Alone I walk gathering fallen leaves,
For it is autumn and the day of the dead.
I come to where in solemn silence broods
A monument to them whose fame still rings
(Clear as a bugle blown) to him that grieves,
And lay my leaves for crown upon each head.
Here, my old Forest friends, are your own flowers!
Beautiful in their death as you in yours;
Symbol of all you loved, and were, and are.
Beautiful now as when you lived among us!
And in their heart I place this spotted fungus,
Symbol of war that slayeth all things fair.

Remembrance Day. Yorkley Cenotaph.

A PARCEL FOR THE TROOPS

Here's wool to mind you of the Cotswold Sheep,
And warm to happy dream your shivering sleep.
Smoke to evoke the memory of mist
Uprising purple, grey and amethyst
O'er rocky Malvern, and that magic bubble
Upon the west – May Hill, and patchwork stubble
Below: Dean chimneys, and each smoky stack
Of towns and villages that wish you back.
A memory of all good English things
That wish you safely back, our parcel brings.
Look for our wishes when
You open what was sent by Gloster men:
Men proud of their own regiment were they once,
But now still prouder since you are its sons.

THE HERALD FLOWERS

Before Spring's army marching comes
With flags a flying and beating drums
Daffodil blowing a golden horn
And bluebells ringing her chimes to the morn.

Before Spring's gaily coloured throng
Comes singing its victorious song;
Snowdrop and crocus (white and gold)
Push heralds' heads against the cold.

Piercing with helm and golden spear
The silver shield of Winter drear.

Hark! those herald flowers sing
"Spring is coming – the Spring! the Spring!

THE OLDEST INHABITANT HEARS FAR OFF THE DRUMS OF DEATH

Sometimes 'tis far off, and sometimes 'tis nigh,
Such drummerdery noises too they be!
'Tis odd – oh, I do hope I baint to die
Just as the summer months be coming on,
And buffly chicken out, and bumble-bee:
Though, to be sure, I cannot hear 'em plain
For this drat row as goes a-drumming on,
Just like a little soldier in my brain.

And oh, I've heard we got to go through flame
And water-floods – but maybe 'tisn't true!
I allus were a-frightened o' the sea.
And burning fires – oh, it would be a shame
And all the garden ripe, and sky so blue.
Such drummerdery noises, too, they be.

SETH BEMOANS THE OLDEST INHABITANT

We heard as we wer passing by the forge:
    "Er's dead", said he.
" 'Tis Providence's doing", so said George.
"He's allus doing summat", so I said,
"You see this pig; we kept un aal the year
Fatting un up and priding in un, see,
And spent a yup o' money – food so dear!
    I wish 'twer 'e;
I'd liefer our fat pig had died than she."

A RIVER, A PIG, AND BRAINS

Last fall, to sell his oldest perry,
Old Willum Fry did cross the ferry,
And thur inside of an old sty
'A seed a leanish pig did lie:
A rakish, active beast 'a was
As ever rooted up the grass:
Eager as bees on making honey
To stuff his self. Bill did decide
To buy un with the cider money
And fat un up for Easter-tide.

He bought un, but no net 'ad got
To kip thic pig inside the boat.
"The'll drown we' pig and all at ferry!"
Cried one. Said Fry, "Go, bring some perry,
And this old drinking-horn you got,
Lying inside the piggery cot!"

He poured a goodish swig and soon
– As lazy as a day o' June –
Piggy lay boozed, and so did bide
Snoring, while him and Fry were taken
'Cross Severn: and 'a didn't waken
Until the boat lay safely tied
Up to a tree on t'other side.

IN PILLOWELL WOODS

(Dedicated to Franz Schubert)

You've seen flame burn
    Blue round the raisins
When children played snapdragon. You have seen
Black drift-wood turn
    To azure that emblazons
Dusk with the sheen
    Of stars awaking, and shaking
A sudden light at night,
In some small sea-shore hut:
Watched blue of flame, of wave, of heaven:– but
Have you not been
    This Spring to Pillowell?
How can you know
    Of azure-magic aught? I have heard tell
That under beeches
No plant will grow; and so
    May be it was not bluebells covering
    And lovering beech roots there,
    But air
On fire with all desire
    Of lovers dead and gone
    Who walked upon
And danced upon such azure;
Or seeking dangerous treasure
    On coloured seas,
In flowery fragrant seas of flaming blue
    Beneath those trees
Were drowned. . . If such be true
    Ask not me but the birds
Whose lovely speeches
    Fair-fashioned without words
Enchant those beeches.

To me they *seemed* like bluebells: millions,
    Nay, myriads of bluebells. . . Their small chiming
Out-rang the peal of all the bells of bronze
    In all the world. But whether 'twas a chiming
For lovers living, or for lovers dead.
Who knows in Pillowell where the bluebells pillow well
    A lover's drowsy head?

DEVIL'S CHAPEL

In Devil's Chapel they dug the Ore
A thousand years ago, and more.
Earth's veins of gleaming metal showing
Like crusted blood first set aglowing
Phœnician faces. Profiteers
No doubt, they bought the toil and tears
Of old Silurian miners. Then
Came Rome with all her marching men:–
The conquering legions: then resounded
Those rocks with cries of slaves sore wounded.
Sword, whip, and spear drew British blood.
So labour's law at last held good.
And of that dark and blood-soaked earth
Daggers and armour came to birth:
Yea, many a sword which cut a throat
In far Imperial Rome . . . Where boat
Could sail, the ore of Dean was taken
And put to use. If but kind bracken
Had covered all from sight, what evil
Born in that Chapel of the devil
Had ne'er been done! 'Tis now a walk
For tourists. There shy lovers talk,
But seldom after dusk; for, though
Love scorns not night's soft cloak, I trow,

Yet love and death are ill to pair,
And murder haunts the forest there.
And murdered men, though they go light,
And show not to the mortal sight,
And sound not in a lover's ear,
Tap at the heart, and put cold fear
Into the blood. The sighing hiss
Of trees or ghosts makes blasphemies
Of words, and poison love's warm kiss.

Yet all to sight is fair as heaven
O'er forest trunks, and great rocks riven,
Embroideries of moss make hues
Varied and bright as morning dews
Whose globed crystals can set free
Light's captive colours. Many a tree
Splinters the sunlight overhead.
The path is softly carpeted
With moss. Fully many a ferny grot
Beckons. – So, like you, or like you *not*,
Builded on this grim haunted spot
A Chapel fine hath the Devil got!

SPRINGTIME AND HARVEST SHALL NOT CEASE

A glitter on the ploughland like glitter on water:
Sun and breeze playing o'er the green young wheat:
Hawthorn a-blowing and scattering spring-laughter:
May-music playing to dancing feet.

Here is the boyhood of the year, the flying
Fleet-footed Youth that follows drum and fife.
Later in the Autumn when golden heads are lying,
The grain of drooping age will renew the earth with life!

SPRING 1924

Spring came by water to Broadoak this year.
 I saw her clear.
Though on the earth a sprinkling
Of snowdrops shone, the unwrinkling
Bright curve of Severn River
Was of her gospel first giver.
Like a colt new put to pasture it galloped on;
And a million
Small things on its back for token
Of her coming it bore. A broken
Hawthorn floated green
Gem-bright upon the sheen
Of the moving water. There past
Hay-wisps which showed the fast
Of winter was over for cattle,
Who needed no longer battle
For food in some far meadow.
Soft as shadow
There glided past a skiff,
Heavy with mended nets for salmon. If
Spring dreamed
Lazily in Earth's half-frozen blood,
On Severn's flood
Her presence bravely gleamed.
Yea, all who sought her
Might see, wondering, how Spring walked the water.

JOHN HELPS

John Helps a wer an honest mon;
    The perry that a made
Wer crunced vrom purs as honest
    As ever tree displayed.

John Helps a wer an honest mon;
    The dumplings that a chewed
Wer made vrom honest apples
    As Autumn ever growed.

John Helps a wer an honest mon,
    And I be sorry a's dead.
Perry and honest men be scarce
    These days, 'tiz zed.

SONG

On Wintry hedges pale buds wait.
    How small a sun
Should crown the world in Springtime state:
    Make sweet song run!

Life longing waits for Love to chase
    This death away.
Oh turn sweet Love thine April face!
    Crown us to-day.

KNOWLEDGE

I know not how the little rills
Are born, nor how the daffodils,
Nor how the steadfast giant hills.

Naught know I of the light fast stored
To fill each golden morrow full;
Naught of those reeds whose whispered word
Turns all the river sorrowful.

And of the source of mortal breath,
And of the cause of human pain,
And of the lonely house of Death,
And of the life things live again,
With certainty I know but this –

That God's keen arrows cannot miss;
That nothing was and nothing is
Too far or small for Love to kiss.

And when these worlds are drifted dust
About the chariot wheels of fate,
This single knowledge shall, I trust,
Survive the brunt of giant wars,
And when the heavens are desolate
Outlast the ruin of the stars.

RAIN AFTER DROUGHT

The earth was dry
    It opened mouths to cry
But could not speak.

The clouds on high
    Looked downwards from the sky
With pity for the weak.

The little mouths gave thanks
    With primroses on banks
And bluebells ringing.

The rain had slaked their throats,
    And flowers were notes
Of their sweet singing.

(For children)

AUTUMN MOOD

The leopard hills lie crouched
    Beneath the lashing rain;
Last leaves with colour touched
    Dapple each wooded flank,
    That shakes with deadly pain.

The ways are dark and dank,
    The leaves and the birds are flying,
See! Clustered rank on rank
    Along the wires, sad swallows
    Grieve for the year that's dying.

The mad wind moans and halloas,
    The flying rain-stroms race;
A sudden sun-gleam follows,
    And flickers like the smile
    That lights a dying face.

"Ah, linger yet awhile,
    Sweet light!" In vain we cry;
"Oh, longer to beguile
    This darkness and despair,
    Wherein all dreams must die."

"All fiery dreams and fair
    That we have dared to dream;
All sunny hours and rare
    We gathered up like flowers;
All blossoming boughs a-gleam
    All joys that once were ours."

TO THE OLD YEAR

Old year, farewell!
Much have you given which was ill to bear:
Much have taken which was dear, so dear:
Much have you spoken which was ill to hear;
Echoes of speech first uttered deep in hell.

Pass now like some grey harlot to the tomb!
Yet die in child-birth, and from out your womb
Leap the young year unsullied! He perchance
Shall bring to man his lost inheritance.

MUST WE FORGET?

Must we forget in the whirl and wheel of the "Age of Steel"
All once we felt:– and feel?
    – Strife, shout and knife
    At throat of quiet life?

Must we forget in the sense's cymbal'd and the buzz-saw's thin
Whine of thought, another within,
    Nor ever find
    The quiet mind?

HILLS

Far and Near

"Lift up your eyes to the hills!"
The heart within me cried.
And I thought on the far blade of Cotswold unscabbarded blue.
"Lift up your eyes to the hills!"
And I dreamed of the uplands wide –
The flock-specked upland sward of the land I knew.

When I, in the Flanders O,
In danger and distress,
Thought on that loveliness
I feared not foe,
Dirt,
Lice,
Nor hurt,
For my heart was high on hill called Paradise.

But now that paradise
Doth fly
Beyond the O of the world,
Beyond its lust, and lies,
And lice,
Cometh again the cry:
"Lift up your eyes to the hills!"
Lift up your heart to the hills!

There to thou shalt never come.
But they are the hills of home,
Whence thy help cometh.
Those hills thou hast never seen,
Nor may, with mortal eyes –
The dim, dear, dreamed-near hills of Paradise.

INCIDENTAL

A face looked out of a tree –
    A smooth face, yet wrinkled.
    Eyes twinkled
Like frosty leaves at me,
As I walked on my way to work through a wood called
    Harp Wood.

I, the flesh and blood;
He, the creature of the wood,
Gazed smiling for a moment each on each.
There was not any speech.
Only I passed to work, and the face of beech
Stayed smiling on within the wood called Harp Wood.

FREE TRAVEL TO FORESTERS!

("In the dark backward and abysm of time")

    Who wonders not is dead.
So all live men are poets though they tarry
In one small village through a life-time:– Wonder
Being a wandering of spirit, a tracing and tracking
Of beauty. One may wander
Beside a stream enjoying every winding
    Till at its source into dark earth
    It vanishes. But long before it rose
It fell in rain, and long before it fell it rose in mist,
    And long, long before rising
    Or falling
It was.
    But once was not:– ah, there's great wonder!

And there's a stream whose ripples are men's lives.
And once was not: nor man nor forefather
Nor ancestor of any kind. The spirit must
Wander in wonder a billion billion years
Tracking a fern shape to its first rough drawing
To grasp the hand that drew, then smudged it out
And drew again, and draws for evermore.

Amid the bracken, beneath the bough
    I sought
And found the thought
I give you now,
That you may *travel free!*
    Goodbye! My fee
I will demand a billion years hence.

CRY HAPPY THINGS

Cry happy things!
    Shout for the sky that launches
A brave ship, tempest scorning:
    A ship of magic gold!

Forget the night's sad wailers,
    Death's bodeful ravens!
Shout, bold sailors,
    Bound for all happy havens!

GOD IN THE FOREST

God dwells in the Forest of Dean.
    And so doth the devil, ha! ha!
Both dwell in the Forest of Dean.

I

In the nipples of hills,
In the ripples of rills,
There thrills and spills
In the Forest of Dean,
Who's glory but Thine?
Thy mysteries shine
On the leaves for a sign
In the Forest of Dean.
They blaze below
Thy bright-hued bow
Bended aglow
In heaven above.
Lest men forget
In fear and fret
    Thy love:
Lest men deride
In hate and pride
    Thee, named Love.

II

Observed, not understood,
Rainbow, and rainbow-wood
Seen WITH, not THROUGH the eye!
Make heart thine eyes, and cry
Aloud for the Forest of Dean!

See now, mid trees,
What the devil sees!
(He dwells in the Forest of Dean.)
Squalor and sin,
They make him grin
In the forest – his Forest of Dean!
He smiles, and he smells
O'er the little white hells,
And the little grey hells,
And the little red hells
Where men bide in the Forest of Dean.
He grins when they go
Through sleet and snow
To labour below
Underground
And be drowned
In the pits of the Forest of Dean.
The wife weeping wild
O'er the fatherless child
He sees in the Forest of Dean.
But it pleaseth him less
Than the devilish mess
Man-made in his Forest of Dean.
Death pleaseth him less
Than a living distress
Wherein all acquiesce
In his forest, the Forest of Dean.

III

Do all acquiesce?
    Say nay!
(God dwells in the Forest of Dean.)
    The leaves, e'en they,
In their loveliness
    Are warriors all.

The croziers small
Of bracken, ban
The pride of man.
Merry blue bells
Ring to all hells,
And holes
For souls
Christ died to save
In His forest – the Forest of Dean.

IV

Arise! Arise from the grave,
To holiness of beauty, and beauty of holiness.
Rise in the armour of your gentleness;
In the rags of your dull misery:
In the strength of god-like patience,
And humour:
Led by your pity for others.
Led by no ranted rumour
Of easy sty-delights, Arise, O brothers

Ye walk not lonely, though alone ye walk.
Ye pray not vainly if to God ye talk.
Ye lie not lonely, though ye lie in hell.
Despair not, but take courage, knowing well
Who goeth with you through the woodland green,
Who goeth always with you – but unseen:
Yea! God in the Forest of Dean.

COAL

(A Sermon)

I sing the dark poetic theme
Of coal that's ripped from out a seam
    (And every man is coal),
And every cinder symbol of
That dark creation of God's love
    (Fire sleeping in his soul).

Fire is (of soul) the blazing coal;
Fire is (of coal) the sleeping soul;
    So man is made of coal.
Colliers and coal conceal the glow
Of sunrise kindled long ago
    And hidden in a hole.

This forest old as we pretend
Is young in years; and when we spend
    Amid its gold and green
Our lives, what deem we of those trees,
The countless, countless ancestries
    That countless suns have seen?

For countless forests one by one
Took the great life-giving sun
    Into their branch and bole
And fell and died (as die we deem)
Until they turned into a seam
    Of hidden, black, hard coal.

That ancient prisoned sunshine is
A symbol of God's mysteries.
    For coal that seemeth dark
As night; when raised with sweat and toil
From its dark dungeon of the soil,
    Preserves its ancient spark.

And collier-men are symbols of
All souls that strive to show the love
    That lights a darkened world.
Black bishops, gloomy deans of Dean,
These show and symbolise, I ween,
    A flag of faith unfurled.

FRIENDLY FURNITURE

Fear not little ones! Let no strange creaking:
No ghostly step or shade, make you dismayed!
'Tis but the friendly furniture that's speaking.

Lamp. I give you light
To read at night
To read and write
In quiet hours.

Clock. I am the clock.
With my tick-tock
I measure time
Before it go:
That you may know
To take the prime
And be not slow.

Fire. I warm the room.
I paint the gloom
With flickering red
Of suns long dead.

Bed. I am the bed
Lay down your head
And take your rest
For sleep is best;
Aye – sleep is best.

Others. We too, we too
Are friends to you!

Table. A tree was I.

Chair. And I.

Sideboard. And I.

All. Gladly we died to bring you ease.
But we remember we *were* trees.

So when at night you hear a creaking
Think only that old trees are speaking:
Let no child be afraid!
Tables and chairs and wooden stairs
All once were young,
In a forest glade
Their branches crowned with stars, or with
Green leafage hung.

HEN AND CHICKENS

Ducks I have praised in song. And Ducks I love.
But why should Ducks have all my praise?
What of –
The fussy hen,
The coloured cock,
The little flock
Of lemon chicks
That cheep and peep around the ricks;
Not greedy like the gobble-ducks
Who care not what they eat,
Not clumsy like the wobble-ducks
On web-toed orange feet,
But delicate and neat
Amid the scattered wheat,
And scornful of the squabble-ducks
Who rudely push and cheat
To gobble mucky meat?

Yes you, my fluffy darlings,
So harmless are and sweet,
You'll share your grain with starlings
And sparrows. Little robin
Comes like a flame bob-bobbin
To join you when you eat.
Should a black crow fly over,
Or should a grey hawk hover,
Swiftly you seek the cover
Of one protecting breast:
Your mother's near to love you,
Her strong wings are above you
And round you for a nest.

You are not comical on earth,
Nor beautiful in water
Like ducks. You move no mirth:
No shout of heavenly laughter.
(What deeper lies than laughter?
Tears. Jesus wept. "If thou
Hadst known. If thou, O city,
Hadst known thy peace! but now
'Tis hidden . . .) Heavenly pity
Speaks
As the downy breast of a hen
Covers her huddled brood. But men
Were Jesus' chicks!

THE FIRE

What's in the fire?
    Speak Youth!
"Beauty, and Love, and Truth,
    Symbols of heart's desire,
    Are in the fire."

Speak of the mid age!
    What's in the fire?
"I see there in a cage
    Of iron – just the fire!
What more should man desire?"

What's in the fire?
    Speak old one!
"Nay, ask not. 'Tis a cold one
    The flick'ring voices tire;
Dead is the fire."

LIFE

Strange and lovely past all telling
Life the bubble gleams,
The bubble shall break, and I awake
To other lovelier dreams.

O let me see while you are here
Let me not go blind!
Nor saying adieu, forget one hue
I must leave behind.

JOYOUS AWAKENING

I am glad to forget . . .
Glad to look out this morning
Upon a world fairer than any dream.
I am glad to forget my dreams.

They were cobwebbed o'er with mortal fret,
Too fearful of Death's warning.
They could not sing for grief – those boding dreams,
I am glad to forget my dreams.

For hark! Joy sings –
A bird on the world's bare branches:
And on this new-made morning
Nothing is tired or old.

FOR EVER

O but it is not the years,
    It is I, it is you:
Our hopes and fears
That fly for ever,
    And cry for ever, winging like birds the blue.

It is not time passes, but men.
    Time stands still.
But beyond ken
Flies on for ever
    And ever, the bird of man's light fluttering will:

His courage, cowardice,
    The joys that thrilled him through.
Time is firm, like ice.
But life, a river,
    Runs on for ever to countries strange and new.

TWO SONNETS

1. The Question

When darkness brims the night: and I, in bed,
Lie half-emeshed in Morphe's net of dreams:
Under a pillow, neath my resting head,
A small watch beats. To me the ticking seems
Like far-heard trotting on a highway lone
Of hoofs; and harkening, suddenly I find
The bed, a big-wheeled trap: and 'Prince', the roan,
My father drove – in shafts: and I behind,
Hiding my head to "guess at where we are"
As children will. And then, the Vision's out.
Father and horse depart: and Time's the mare
That trots us bravely through the night no doubt!
But "whither?" and "who drives?", I question, "Come,
The truth, thou coachman, speak!" But he is dumb.

2. The Reply

With steady pace trots on Time's phantom steed,
Her ghostly driver, sleeping or awake,
Sits at our elbow; but he does not heed
Our cries, nor tell us of the road we take.
But I, still mindful of a happy child
That built fine castles underneath the rugs,
The while his father, driving, sat and smiled;
And falling moonbeams fingered – o'er the tugs,
And burnished up their buckles into fire;
Trust that to-day, as in the days behind,
The gig is homeward-bound thro' all the mire.
And, playing still in darkness, call to mind
That He Who guides the hour, and rules the tide,
Has made the words "Our Father" to abide.

ABSOLUTION

Empty thy memory of evil done.
    Remorse's dagger pluck from out thy heart.
    Grieve not for what thou art,
Kneeling upon the silver grass before the sun.

And while thy knees do stain
    Darkly the innocent grass,
    Empty thy soul as 'twere a poisoned glass
Of all that therein is of old contentment, or pain.

Then from the awful beauty of a world
    Virgin to-day as at creation, take
    That healing absolution which can shake
Heart's burning thirst, and loosen the long snake curled

About thy life . . . Look up!
    Swords of the sun shall pierce thee through and through,
    Yet slay thee not: and (brighter than the dew)
Thy tears shall leave thee empty as a cup:–

A chalice fashioned for nothing else than this
    Same innocent beauty: yea Earth's earliest dream,
    Which even now doth gleam
Glorious with old wonder and holy mysteries.

The dawn shall be thy priest; and thou shalt go
    Fearlessly back into a world of time,
    Mailed with the magic of thy golden prime:–
Peace immortal and pardon upon thy mortal brow.

TIME AND I

Time has tugged my teeth away:
Thinned my hair and turned it grey:
Killed my friends: and will kill me.
Yet Time is not my enemy.

Time on his appointed way
Goeth as I on mine today:
Goeth onward with a sigh,
Grumbling maybe as do I.

Goeth maybe glad of heart
To have been and seen a part
Of this world's proud pageantry
Time's an actor just like me.

Wondering; – waiting his last cue –
"Exit" – (just like I, and you)
As theatre lights fade out
What the play was all about!

LAMENT

The purple plums lie scattered on the ground
Under the garden hedge where sun has etched
Outline of Prune and Damson tree, and sketched
Grasses in thin dark shadow. A sweet sound
Of windy whispering runs the garden round.

Lines of high-clambering rainbow-tinted peas,
With coloured butterflies that seem as if
Those flowers were taking wing, are here: and stiff
Still soldier-pea-sticks, heeding not the breeze
That shakes to merriment the Damson-trees,

So that they fling their fruit for very mirth
(Small dusky plums) around me as I sit
Pondering with a wasted love and wit
The old Earth's sweetness, and that mortal worth
Buried beneath the beauty of the Earth:

Because the utter sweetness of this ground
Comes of a strength and sweetness hidden there –
The golden lads, and girls beyond compare
In beauty: and they speak in every sound
Of this old garden when the wind goes round.

DEAD MEN'S EYES

These shapes of hills, fold upon wooded fold;
A road bent like a dog's hind leg, and a road
That writhes like a twisting worm, and the white broad
Marching road of the Romans –
            I behold
I see them with two eyes, but with eyes more old
Than are in this head. What men of flesh they were
First looked upon this land and found it fair
            Who knows?
And who can guess their manifold
Longings and services paid back with death?

Only I know they did not grudge the price
Because their hearts were filled with some wild fire,
That flickered on till the last sobbing breath,
Only I know dead men have lent me eyes
Or borrowed mine for sake of old desire.

LOVERS GOODBYE

Lover's goodbye!
I cannot stay
To linger out at dusty day,
There is soft sleep beneath the yew
Whose lamps burn red above my head,
I need no ray to light the way–
All ways are ended. I am dead.
'Tis from the grave I call to you,
    Lovers goodbye.

DEAD MAN

I had always wanted a chance
    Better than life could give:
I have got it – (let no one grieve!)
    My long inheritance.